A Survival Guide to

THE
STRESS OF
ORGANIZATIONAL
CHANGE

Price Pritchett & Ron Pound

PRITCHETT

STRESS:
THE INVISIBLE EPIDEMIC

Antibiotics can't touch it. The microscope can't even spot it. It's rapidly spreading, and almost everybody's feeling the effect.

Stress is the hot word these days.

Most people seem to agree that these are high pressure times. Employees complain of being burned out. Used up. Overloaded. Too many of us are just plain tired, overdosed on change, sick of ambiguity and uncertainty.

And if today's stress and tension aren't enough to create problems, all a person has to do is consider what the future holds. One close look at what's in store should be enough to worry anyone.

Actually today is just a warmup. Tomorrow promises us an even more complex world, a still faster rate of change, and—unless we learn to handle life better—more stress than we ever dreamed of. These soon will be remembered as "the good old days."

Most of us just wish that change would go away. Or at least slow down. When it doesn't, we look around for someone to blame it on, or for someone we think should be responsible for relieving our stress.

But since higher management has its hands full these days, we're probably not going to get much emotional hand-holding from those folks. We also can't count on the world giving us much of a breather. What we can do, though, is be a lot more clever in the way we manage our own behavior.

Instead of behaving in ways that actually create stress for ourselves, let's get better at adapting. If we can't change the situation, we can at least make big changes in the way we handle it.

PRITCHETT

TABLE OF CONTENTS

3 "KEY DRIVERS" OF CHANGE

W e could identify a wide range of factors that are reshaping our world and the way we live. But let's focus on three major forces.

PEOPLE

Here's the most obvious reason why we'll see an even faster rate of change in the years to come: Mother Earth is producing a lot more people. And people cause change. Like, they make stuff. They come up with new ideas. They compete for scarce resources. Whatever sorts of things people do, we'll see happening more and faster.

Some hard statistics will help make the point.

Human beings have been around for maybe 7,000,000 years, but the population of our planet didn't reach a billion until the early 1860's, about the time of the Civil War. Within the short span of a mere 75 years, though, the head count doubled, to two billion. Then, by 1975 it doubled again, to four billion—this time in only 40 years. Today we're closing in on six billion, with U.S. Census statistics predicting a world population of ten billion by the year 2040.

TECHNOLOGY

Since technology is a product of the human race, we can expect the rate of technological change to follow the trends in population growth. And that is precisely what's been going on.

It is said that well over 80% of the world's technological advances have occurred since 1900. With still more people to come—and also because technology actually feeds on itself—a rapidly accelerating rate of technological change is basically guaranteed.

INFORMATION

The third powerful force driving change is information. Knowledge.

Get this. There was more information produced in the 30 years between 1965 and 1995 than was produced in the entire 5,000-year period from 3000 B.C. to 1965. Word has it that the amount of information available in the world is doubling every five years. Plus, all this knowledge and information is becoming available to many more people than it ever reached before.

Far more knowledge, reaching far more people, far faster than ever before. Bottom line? A better informed population means better chances for change.

So look out! If "change" and "stress" are connected—and they are—life isn't going to get any easier.

"The world bats last."

— Anonymous

COMING TO GRIPS WITH REALITY

This rapidly changing world demands a higher level of adaptability. New moves. Our old reaction patterns will bring us nothing but problems.

THE DANGER OF DOING WHAT COMES NATURALLY

We can look around and see many would-be refugees from change, people looking for easy relief from all the stress. Yet there is no place to run. No back door. No escape route from reality.

There are also many fierce and noble warriors making a fateful stand, struggling against the relentless advance of change. But however valiant and determined they might be, theirs is a wrong and futile fight. The world, as always, will have its way.

Neither "fight" nor "flight"—our bodies' instinctive choices in response to stress—offers much promise of a lasting solution to the situation. Instead, we must find another alternative. Something that works. Something that serves us well in this world of high-velocity change.

The secret is surrender. That's the only way to win.

THE ZEN WAY

Surrendering to change does the most to eliminate the stress. It creates the opportunity for breakthrough rather than breakdown.

The Zen masters of Eastern cultures had great respect for the power of submission. They knew that to yield—to give in to a situation—sometimes offers the only pathway to mastery. They would speak of the wisdom in letting the world have its way . . . of going with change rather than against it. Then instead of being "stressed out" by change, we turn its power to our advantage. Its strength becomes ours.

So instead of seeing change as an adversary, we should accommodate it . . . align with it . . . use it. Rather than treating it like an enemy, we should allow it to become our greatest ally.

PLAYING THE HAND THAT LIFE DEALS US

To be effective in this new day and age, we've got to know when to "give up" . . . that is, when to surrender to change.

Beyond that, though, we've got to toughen up. Circumstances are simply going to require us to develop a higher tolerance for stress.

Finally, we've got to wise up. We must pay attention to how we're making life more difficult for ourselves. Too much of the pressure we're feeling these days is self-induced stress, the result of basic mistakes we're making in how we react to change.

The following chapters highlight the destructive behaviors we must abandon, and also offer guidelines that equip us for survival and success during these times of high-velocity change.

"Reality is something you rise above."

— Liza Minnelli

BASIC MISTAKE #1 EXPECT SOMEBODY ELSE TO REDUCE YOUR STRESS.

We know that change commonly causes stress. Okay . . . so who's causing the changes?

Usually higher management takes the rap. After all, the people at the top call the shots. So on the surface it seems fair to accuse them of being a main source of the emotional strain and pressure. Plus, if upper management's actions seem to be the problem, doesn't it make sense to hold them responsible for providing the solution?

No. For several reasons.

To begin with, appearances can be deceiving. The top management moves are often reactions.

Chances are, the organization is simply trying to respond to some outside force. Maybe stiffer competition. Sharp economic turns. New technology. Or shifts in the marketplace and customer expectations. If management is simply trying to deal with a more basic, underlying problem that threatens the organization's future, then that root cause is the real culprit.

But suppose this line of reasoning hits you as a rather weak defense for management. Maybe in your opinion it doesn't get them off the hook.

Let's say, for instance, that you believe somebody made a bad call. You think there was a better way of handling the situation. With that in mind, you insist that somebody else caused unnecessary stress, and so they should bear the burden of protecting you against it.

What if they don't?

To fix the situation—to get rid of the stress—the organization would have to change things. But they just did—for reasons, and in ways, that probably make sense from their point of view. It's not likely top management sees it as a mistake. Apparently, this is the way they want it, considering the options they have available. In fact, any further changes are likely to create even more stress, not less.

SURVIVAL GUIDE:

Don't count on anybody else
coming along to relieve
your stress.
Put *yourself* in charge of
managing the pressure.
There's a good chance
you're the only one
in your work situation
who will,
or even *can*,
do much to lighten
your psychological load.

" Have I reached the person to whom I am speaking? "

— Lily Tomlin as "Ernestine"

BASIC #2 MISTAKE 2 DECIDE NOT TO CHANGE.

You don't have to change just because the organization does. People prove this all the time. Just look around—maybe even glance in the mirror. You won't have to look far to find what we're talking about.

Here's how it goes. The organization announces that it will do something new and different. Some people don't like the looks of it, for whatever reasons, and decide they don't want any part of the program.

So they resist. Maybe consciously, or maybe without really stopping to think about it. Maybe they make a lot of noise and fight out in the open. Or maybe they take the sneaky approach and fight the changes quietly and behind the scenes. Whichever strategy they choose, though, they set themselves up for a tough emotional struggle.

Resisting change is one of the most common causes of stress on the job. And it's stress that we bring on ourselves. Naturally, the average person doesn't see it that way. Most folks like to think the changes give birth to all the stress, rather than blaming their own mistakes in how they personally react to the situation.

The truth of the matter? People waste far more emotional energy desperately hanging on to old habits and beliefs than it would take for them to embrace the changes.

People also do a lousy job of weighing the odds for success when they resist change. Most of the time they're fighting a lost cause.

For example, does it make sense to assume that we can remain effective in a changing organization without changing ourselves? If the world is forcing organizations to do business differently, can we as individuals expect to succeed if we keep going at our jobs in the same old way?

Don't forget that you have a choice. Maybe you don't like the options you have to pick from, but you have a say-so in how you react to change.

SURVIVAL GUIDE:

The organization is going to change—it *must*—
if it is to survive and prosper.
Rather than banging your head
against the wall of hard reality
and bruising your spirit,
invest your energy
in making quick adjustments.
Turn when the organization turns.
Practice instant alignment.
Your own decisions may do more to
determine your stress level
than anything the organization
decides to do.

"Ride the horse in the direction that it's going."

— Werner Erhard

Basic Mistake #3   Act Like a Victim.

Stress ratchets up fast if you decide that you're helpless. Just convince yourself there's not much you can do about the situation, and see how much worse you feel.

The idea here is to consider yourself a victim of circumstances. Emphasize the unfairness of it all. Play "poor me." Ignore any opportunities the changes might imply. Focus instead on what's being lost, on any sacrifices you must make. Assume if you feel sorry enough for yourself, other people will start feeling sorry for you as well.

You'll also be a better victim if you find somebody else to blame, someone you can accuse of causing your problems. If you can pull that off, you shift the accountability for your behavior and attitude away from yourself.

Pretty slick move?

You'll see people try such maneuvers all the time. The problem is, this is very disempowering stuff we do to ourselves. It happens almost unconsciously. The irony is that we do it in our defense, and it ends up doing us all kinds of personal damage.

Any time we act like a victim, we actually weaken ourselves. We load ourselves down with more self-induced stress. Beyond that, we set ourselves up as an even more likely candidate for future victimization, because we literally make ourselves more expendable. Our public suffering makes us much less appealing as an employee.

This is stress that perpetuates itself. We end up in a vicious circle, and we're the only ones that can break ourselves free.

Survival Guide:

Accept fate, and move on.
Don't yield to the
seductive pull of self-pity,
at least for any extended period of time.
Acting like a victim threatens your future.
You're better off if you
appear resilient and remain productive.
Just stand proud,
pick up the pieces,
and start putting
your career back together.

"I feel so bad since you've gone. It's almost like having you here."

— Anonymous

BASIC MISTAKE #4 — TRY TO PLAY A NEW GAME BY THE OLD RULES.

Many people make the mistake of trying harder instead of trying differently. They realize their work situation is changing and, in an attempt to cope, they react as if more effort is the answer.

But trying harder won't take you very far if you're failing to do the right things. "More of the same" may just add stress and tension.

We need to respect the fact that our rapidly changing world requires actual changes—big changes—in our work behavior. Most jobs are taking on totally new dimensions . . . making new demands . . . calling for new work habits. Maybe you think it's stressful having to make all the necessary adjustments. But if you think adapting is tough duty, just see how difficult life becomes if you don't.

Struggling to do a job in ways that aren't working really wears on your nerves. It's like a car stuck in second gear that's trying to hit speeds over 100 miles per hour. Pretty soon the stress and strain cause engine damage.

We must be willing to alter our technique. Rather than barrelling ahead with the same old job behaviors that worked well enough in the past, we must learn new routines. And we must make the necessary shift in our mindset so that our thinking is aligned with the new realities of the work world.

Organizations are developing a very different set of expectations regarding job performance and employee attitudes. We need to pay close attention. We can avoid a lot of work pressure if we'll simply play by the new rules.

SURVIVAL GUIDE:

Study the situation intently.
Figure out how the game has changed,
how priorities have been reordered.
Decide which aspects of your job
you should focus on
to leverage up
your effectiveness
the most.

*"The other day I got out my can-opener and was opening
a can of worms when I thought, 'What am I doing?!'"*

— Jack Handey, *Deepest Thoughts* from "Saturday Night Live"

BASIC MISTAKE #5   SHOOT FOR A LOW-STRESS WORK SETTING.

How safe is it really to assume that a low-stress work environment serves our best interests?

Let's say we push for a slower pace of change . . . less pressure to perform . . . a more relaxed, low-keyed atmosphere in general. And let's say we prevail. Top management cuts us some slack.

Chances are we enjoy some temporary relief. Our stress level drops, and maybe we point to that as proof that the organization made the right move.

We'd probably be drawing the wrong conclusion.

There's a lot more evidence these days to suggest that slow-changing organizations are headed for the most trouble. Sure, we can do things to minimize stress for today—we can buy a little time—but we have to mortgage the future. We actually end up living closer to the edge.

It's pretty obvious to people that the stress of a rapidly changing organization can be difficult and unpleasant. What's not so clear to us sometimes is how much more trouble we're in for if the organization fails to change. It just means denying the problems and delaying the pain. All we're actually doing is postponing tough times for tougher times.

Given the choice, which is really in your best interests: being part of an outfit that's struggling with all the stress and problems of progress, or feeling good (for the moment) and failing?

You can pick your poison. But the hard truth is that the stress of high-velocity change is here to stay.

SURVIVAL GUIDE:

Don't fall into the trap of
believing there's such a thing
as a low-stress organization that's
on track to survive.
In fact, just the opposite is true.
You serve your best interests
by aligning with an outfit
that's got the guts to endure
the pains of change,
and by avoiding those organizations
destined to go belly-up
because of their desire for
short-term comfort.

*"The reason lightning doesn't strike twice in the same place
is that the same place isn't there the second time."*

— Willie Tyler

MISTAKE BASIC #6 TRY TO CONTROL THE UNCONTROLLABLE.

S ome employees get all worked up trying to influence matters that lie beyond their reach.

These are the people who resist the inevitable. Who keep trying to undo things that can't be undone. Who act as though they might be able to push change back into the bottle. Or who struggle with matters that lie entirely within someone else's domain.

These people cause themselves high frustration and chronic stress by overstepping their ability to affect the situation.

Some things we just need to accept. Sometimes the real wisdom lies in resigning ourselves to a situation, even if we don't like it. Rather than scratch and claw in a futile effort to control the uncontrollable, we should salute reality and get on with our lives.

Of course, human nature being what it is, we're inclined to "go down fighting." When we feel like we're losing control over our careers—or when an unsteady work world makes us feel like the earth is shifting beneath our feet—we grab almost anything in an attempt to stabilize the situation. The more we feel like we're losing our grip on things, the more we struggle for influence and control.

Just the same, trying to control matters that we personally can't control is a pure waste of time. It's a bad investment of our psychological energy. It also weakens our ability to deal with other issues where our efforts could produce a real payoff.

SURVIVAL GUIDE:

Ask yourself if the struggle makes sense.
Are you really in a position
to control the situation,
or will you just get
emotionally tired trying?
Sometimes the most mature,
most dignified,
and most sensible move
is to nobly accept
what we can't change.

"If the people don't want to come out to the park, nobody's gonna stop them."

— Yogi Berra

BASIC MISTAKE #7 — CHOOSE YOUR OWN PACE OF CHANGE.

S ome people fully intend to accept change, they just want to adapt according to their own schedule.

These folks cooperate . . . up to a point. They really don't mean to resist change, but they do want to stay in their comfort zone. Their plan is to minimize stress by "pacing themselves."

This behavior is based on several faulty assumptions.

First of all, let's examine the mistake that comes in assuming we'll feel less stress if we move slowly to change. Sure, we might—but not if we're falling further behind with every day that passes. Not if our employer starts putting more heat on us because we're bogging down the rest of the organization.

Still another wrong assumption is in thinking we have the privilege of choosing almost any rate of change that "feels right" personally. Frankly, the organization can't give its blessing to that kind of behavior. Some people, given their preference, would take forever to adapt.

We can call ourselves cooperative. We can even give ourselves credit for not deliberately resisting change. But our thinking is badly off key, and we're headed for trouble, if we're not changing as fast as the world around us.

The simple fact is that failure to keep up with the organization's rate of change is resistance. Intent is not the issue here. Impact is. We might be innocent so far as our motives are concerned, but we're guilty of resisting change whenever we slow things down. We also create tension between ourselves and the rest of the organization.

SURVIVAL GUIDE:

Keep in step with
the organization's intended rate of change.
March to the cadence
that's being called
by the people in charge,
instead of allowing yourself to take
whatever amount of time
you want or feel you need.
Don't lag behind—
there's little chance a lull will come along
and give you a chance
to play catch-up.

"You belong to a small, select group of confused people."

— Message in fortune cookie

BASIC#8
MISTAKE

FAIL TO ABANDON THE EXPENDABLE.

J obs seem to grow more complicated every year.

Employees are expected to carry a heavier workload, meet higher quality standards, and pick up speed at the same time. It's a foolproof formula for stress.

Since organizations are under so much pressure from changes in the outside world, though, we can't look forward to any letup. More work keeps landing on fewer shoulders. Customer expectations keep going up. And ever stiffer competition means we have to move faster and faster just to keep up.

Nevertheless, there are limits to the workload we can carry. Trying harder and harder can only take us so far.

If we keep taking on new duties without giving others up, we'll eventually hit overload. This means we should sort through our work, reorder our priorities, and figure out which tasks are expendable. Something has to go. Unless we dump some old baggage, we won't be able to shoulder the more important stuff that offers a bigger payoff.

This isn't as easy as it sounds. People have a funny way of hanging on to old habits. In particular, we're often unwilling to quit doing what we can do well, even if it's no longer the most important thing for us to spend our time on.

You don't have to look very far to find employees who are focused on doing things right, but who are failing to do the right things. These are the people who act as if they'll be held accountable for their old jobs, when—in large part—those assignments don't even exist anymore. Often they just can't understand why they're no longer getting accolades, even though they're doing their old jobs as well as ever. Their key mistake comes in ignoring how priorities and management expectations have changed.

We need to abandon the expendables, because that creates valuable space. Not only does it relieve a lot of the pressure, but it also makes room for the far more important work that higher management is going to grade us on.

SURVIVAL GUIDE:

Reengineer your job.
Eliminate unnecessary steps,
get rid of busywork,
and unload activities that don't
contribute enough
to the organization's current goals.
Focus your efforts on
doing "the right things."
And ditch those duties
that don't count much,
even if you can do them
magnificently right.

"You can't have everything. Where would you put it?"

— Stephen Wright

BASIC MISTAKE #9 SLOW DOWN.

Everyone agrees that change keeps picking up speed. But many people fail to notice how they instinctively slow down in their efforts to cope.

Does this make sense?

Here we are, facing an accelerating rate of change. The job demands keep stacking up on us. There's not much chance that the world will back off, or that our organization will start expecting less of us. If anything, the odds are better that the pressure will continue to build.

Still, whenever we get slammed by another change, our first impulse is to slow down . . . proceed more cautiously . . . buy some time so we can size up the situation. Obviously, we can't do much about the speed of change in the world around us. The only way we can slow things down is to reduce the pace at which we personally proceed.

So our natural reaction is to pull back. Play it safe. Attempt to minimize the risk.

On the surface this makes sense. A more careful analysis of the situation, though, suggests that in the longer run this sort of reaction leads to even greater stress.

Carried to the extreme, some people's attempts to exercise caution reach the point of paralysis. They freeze. Like a deer caught in the glare of a car's headlights, they do nothing. Before long, of course, reality hits.

We can't afford to react to change in a way that lets us fall further and further behind. Rather than rely on our impulses, we have to use our heads.

SURVIVAL GUIDE:

Speed up.
Cover more ground.
Put your faith
in action—in mobility—and maximize
your personal productivity.

"Half this game is 90% mental."

— Danny Ozark, Philadelphia Phillies Manager

BASIC MISTAKE #10 BE AFRAID OF THE FUTURE.

The events of recent years have left a lot of people troubled about tomorrow.

Employees worry about what's coming next, and how they might be affected. They wonder if they'll measure up to the demands of change. Will they become part of the body count in the next round of personnel cuts? And if they do, how will they manage to get their careers back on track?

This is heavy duty stuff to think about.

Carrying around such concerns wears us down. It's like we're dragging an anchor behind us every day when we head toward the job. So much of our energy is spent on this emotional labor that we end up with a short supply to invest in our actual work. We go home drained and dispirited, but our weariness isn't all because of the physical demands we face. A big part of our fatigue can be blamed on stress.

Regardless of how we feel at the end of the day, though, worry is not the same as working. We can bust our tails brooding about the future. We can put in a hard day's labor imagining the worst. But no matter how you slice it, we've wasted all that energy. There's nothing good we get in return.

You just can't build a decent argument for giving in to fear of the future. All it amounts to is borrowing trouble. Sure, the concerns are legitimate enough. But that doesn't mean you should let them squeeze all the juice out of your job.

Survival Guide:

Now's the time for
some serious mind control.
Instead of worrying about
bad things that might happen,
get busy trying to
create the kind of future you want.
The best insurance policy
for tomorrow is
to make the
most productive use of today.

*"If you define cowardice as running away at the first sign of danger,
screaming and tripping and begging for mercy, then yes,
Mister Brave Man, I guess I am a coward."*

— Jack Handey, *Deep Thoughts* from "Saturday Night Live"

BASIC MISTAKE #11 PICK THE WRONG BATTLES.

People going through organizational change often end up with a bad case of battle fatigue.

Some wear themselves out waging war on too many fronts. These are the crusaders in the anti-change crowd, the ones who oppose almost every move the organization makes toward doing things differently. They're always bucking the odds, even fighting for things that actually wouldn't be in their best interests if they managed to get their way. Sooner or later, these nay-sayers end up across the battlefield from the boss, at odds with a person they need as their ally.

Others waste too much emotional energy fighting over trivial issues. They blow things out of proportion, giving major attention to minor problems. For these people, practically no issue is so small that it deserves to be ignored.

Finally, we find the folks who set themselves up for stress and failure by pursuing a lost cause. These are the employees who are determined to "defend the undefendable." They throw themselves across the tracks in a hopeless attempt to stop the freight train of reality. You'll see them arguing against decisions that are irreversible. Or lining up on the losing side where there's no hope of winning.

All this behavior requires enormous amounts of emotional labor. But in spite of all the effort, the end result is more likely to be personal damage than any psychic relief or satisfaction.

Pick the wrong battles, and you put yourself on a sure road to burnout.

SURVIVAL GUIDE:

Remember
the advice
of Jonathan Kozol—
"Pick battles
big enough to matter,
small enough to win."

*"If you are losing a tug-of-war with a tiger,
give him the rope before he gets to your arm.
You can always buy a new rope."*

— Max Gunther

Basic Mistake #12   Psychologically Unplug From Your Job.

T he hassles of high-velocity change are hard on job
commitment.

People get fed up with the situation. Disgusted and demoralized, doubtful about their job security, or just plain tired, they end up basically doing only what it takes to get by. They react to the stress and strain by emotionally disconnecting from their work.

Now it may be that employees are putting in more hours than before. They might argue that they're working harder than ever. But the "blahs" are a common side effect of times like these. People grit their teeth and keep going, but there's no fire. No passion. They work with a resigned sense of "have to" instead of any "want to." Their souls sleep on the job.

It's understandable how we might slip into this behavior pattern. We need to realize, however, that it can only do further damage to our emotional health.

When our heart goes out of our work, life starts to lose its sparkle. Job pressures weigh heavier. And we're even more vulnerable to stress than we were before.

So we really can't afford to quit caring.

High job commitment serves as an excellent antidote to stress. Like some modern wonder drug, commitment makes us emotionally stronger. Happier. Even more secure in our jobs. That's powerful stuff, and well worth the effort that's involved.

Survival Guide:

Fall in love with your job,
and keep the romance alive.
Don't let the stress of change
drive a wedge between
you and your work.
Sure, your employer will benefit
if you're committed,
but not as much as you will.
High job commitment
is a gift you should give
to yourself.

"I started out with nothing. I still have most of it."

— Michael Davis on the "Tonight Show"

BASIC MISTAKE #13 AVOID NEW ASSIGNMENTS.

S ome of us try to minimize stress by shying away from new, unfamiliar duties. Sticking with the work we know just sounds easier.

Really, shouldn't there be less emotional strain involved if we don't have to break our routines?

Sounds reasonable enough.

But this is a short-sighted strategy for managing personal stress. At best it's just a delaying tactic, buying comfort today at tomorrow's expense. At worst it paints a bull's-eye on our backs, making us prime targets for bigger problems in the future.

If we shy away from new assignments, we treat organizational change like it's a spectator sport. Sure, we'll learn something about this "game" just by watching it. But our learning curve is too slow when we stay on the sideline. We can't grow and improve fast enough when we're mainly onlookers.

Only by plunging in—readily accepting tough new assignments—do we pick up the all-important experience we need. It means more job pressure at the outset, but without "game time" we're going to lose our edge. We won't be able to compete in the job market. And the real stress hits if we end up badly out of shape for an even tougher game in the future.

One final point—don't assume that it's less stressful to "ease into" a new situation. Instead of building up your nerve before entering the game, build it by entering the game. One of the best ways to reduce stress is to get better . . . quicker. And, again, you don't get better fast on the sideline.

SURVIVAL GUIDE:

Stretch yourself today
so you'll be in better shape tomorrow.
Reach for new assignments
that broaden your experience base.
Remember that one of the
best techniques for stress prevention
is to keep updating
your skills
so you're highly employable.

"You ought to take the bull between the teeth."

— Samuel Goldwyn

BASIC MISTAKE #14 — TRY TO ELIMINATE UNCERTAINTY AND INSTABILITY.

S truggling to stabilize an ever-changing work world takes a lot out of a person.

It's sort of like trying to sweep water uphill. You can give it everything you've got, but the minute you stop to catch your breath you lose control of the situation again.

We're living in a very fluid situation. Naturally, some people handle all the ambiguity and uncertainty better than others. If you have a high tolerance for this kind of stuff, then the instability may seem like no big deal. But if you're bothered by a blurry future or a fuzzy work role, times like these are bound to be stressful. If you feel a strong need for closure—for things to be "finished"—the unsettled nature of today's world will probably drive you nuts. If you can't stand confusion and change, you'll probably burn yourself out trying to bring order and constancy to a situation where they can't possibly survive.

Today has a very "temporary" quality about it. Predictability is passé, vague is vogue. The ability to improvise has become an essential skill. We must learn to bob and weave. To bounce whenever change hits. To pivot . . . flex . . . operate in a fog. Instead of futilely trying to stabilize the situation, we must learn to exploit instability.

Frankly, we'd be in big trouble if we did get things settled once and for all. In a rapidly changing world, rigidity is a death sentence for careers.

Still, many employees seem to think that if only they can stabilize the situation, they'll feel less stress. The reality? They can't . . . and they wouldn't.

SURVIVAL GUIDE:

Develop a greater tolerance
for constant changes in the game plan.
For mid-course corrections.
For raw surprise.
Allow a little more confusion in your life.
Be willing to feel your way along, to "wing it."
Think of your job as having
movable walls—flex to fit the immediate
demands of the situation,
instead of struggling
to make the job adapt to you.

*"This life is a test; it is only a test. If it were a real life,
you would receive instructions on
where to go and what to do."*

— Unknown

BASIC MISTAKE #15 — ASSUME "CARING MANAGEMENT" SHOULD KEEP YOU COMFORTABLE.

O ne of the ideas that gets tossed around a lot these days suggests that employees are entitled to "caring management." Also, organizations themselves are supposedly best served when they demonstrate that they care for their people.

Let's not argue these points for the time being. Let's just pin down what we're talking about here. Take this whole idea of "caring." What are we really talking about? What does it look like in real life?

Too many people confuse the issues by getting careless in their definitions. They interpret "caring" to mean operating within the boundaries of employees' comfort zones. The argument goes like this: "If management really cared, they'd show it in the way they act. People would come first. Feelings would count. They'd be making it easier on employees, not harder."

According to this line of reasoning, "caring management" would be making life less stressful. Not more. There would be fewer re-organizations. Smaller downsizings. More stability. Employees would enjoy greater job security, ample resources, and—for Pete's sake—a slower pace of change.

But while minimizing job stress may sound like a "caring" move, it's a cruel option in this day and age. Keeping employees comfortable ultimately proves to be one of the most heartless things management could possibly do.

Plus, let's remember that management also should be caring toward stockholders. Toward customers. Employees aren't the only people the organization has to consider.

Today, management can best show it cares by doing what works. By getting results. By attacking change head-on, and doing what the organization must do to survive in this age of instability.

"Caring management" is best defined by the end result. When all is said and done, do you still have an organization that's alive, that's able to meet payroll, that can provide you a job . . . a chance?

Survival isn't necessarily a comfortable process. But it sure beats the alternative.

SURVIVAL GUIDE:

Be careful in what you use
as evidence to evaluate how much
the organization cares about people.
High stress and heavy pressure
may provide the best proof
that management's heart
is in the right place.
All things considered,
trying to keep you comfortable
could be
the most cold-blooded
management
move of all.

*"Sometimes I get the feeling that the whole world is against me,
but deep down I know that's not true.
Some of the smaller countries are neutral."*

— Robert Orben

TAKING PERSONAL RESPONSIBILITY FOR STRESS REDUCTION

B asically this handbook is about prevention. It tells how to handle your work life in ways that keep job stress from becoming a critical problem.

Obviously, prevention is better than having to come up with a cure. But just the same, it makes sense to review the commonly accepted guidelines for reducing stress once it occurs.

15 STEPS TO LOWER STRESS

1. Invest thirty minutes in vigorous physical exercise, three to five times per week (assuming your doctor doesn't have a problem with that). Work up a sweat.
2. Learn relaxation techniques.
3. Cut down on caffeine.
4. Eat right.
5. Meditate. Get still. "Center."
6. Develop better time management habits.
7. Play. Have fun. Recharge.
8. Get plenty of sleep.
9. Smile more. Laugh. Use humor to lighten your emotional load.
10. Count your blessings—daily. Make thankfulness a habit.
11. Say nice things when you talk to yourself.
12. Simplify.
13. Set personal goals. Give yourself a sense of purpose.
14. Forgive. Grudges are too heavy to carry around.
15. Practice optimism and positive expectancy. Hope is a muscle—develop it.

"Patient, Heal Thyself"

These suggestions probably sound very familiar—maybe even trite—to the point that we don't take them very seriously.

Take exercise, for example. Study after study proves that this is Mother Nature's number one treatment for stress and tension. It truly is a "magic bullet." But too many of us just don't want to go through the drill of daily exercise.

Basically, we want stress to go away, but we don't want to have to work at it. Rather than put forth the personal discipline needed to follow these guidelines for stress reduction, we want higher management to "fix it" for us. Specifically, we want them to stop the constant changes that give rise to so much stress.

But let's be honest with ourselves. The tide of events is too big for top management to turn it back. Considering the rapid population growth, technological gains, and increase in information, nobody is in a position to stop organizational change.

So rather than carry on about how others are failing to lower our stress level, let's just make sure we're doing what we ourselves can do.

"Looks like the upper hand is on the other foot."

– Lloyd Bridges, in "Hot Shots! Part Deux"

Books by PRITCHETT, LP

- *After the Merger: The Authoritative Guide for Integration Success**

- *Business As UnUsual: The Handbook for Managing and Supervising Organizational Change**

- *Carpe Mañana: 10 Critical Leadership Practices for Managing Toward the Future*

- *Culture Shift: The Employee Handbook for Changing Corporate Culture**

- *The Employee Guide to Mergers and Acquisitions**

- *The Employee Handbook for Organizational Change**

- *The Employee Handbook for Shaping Corporate Culture: The Mission Critical Approach to Culture Integration and Culture Change**

- *The Employee Handbook of New Work Habits for a Radically Changing World**

- *The Employee Handbook of New Work Habits for The Next Millennium: 10 Ground Rules for Job Success*

- *The Ethics of Excellence*

- *Fast Growth: A Career Acceleration Strategy*

- *Firing Up Commitment During Organizational Change**

- *Hard Optimism: Developing Deep Strengths for Managing Uncertainty, Opportunity, Adversity, and Change**

- *High-Velocity Culture Change: A Handbook for Managers**

• *The Leadership Engine: Building Leaders at Every Level,**
Based on Noel Tichy and Eli Cohen's best-selling hardcover from HarperBusiness, a division of HarperCollins Publishers. Introduction by Price Pritchett.

• *Making Mergers Work: A Guide to Managing Mergers and Acquisitions**

• *Managing Sideways: A Process-Driven Approach for Building the Corporate Energy Level and Becoming an "Alpha Company"**

• *The Mars Pathfinder Approach to "Faster-Better-Cheaper": Hard Proof From the NASA/JPL Pathfinder Team on How Limitations Can Guide You to Breakthroughs*

• *Mergers: Growth in the Fast Lane**

• *MindShift: The Employee Handbook for Understanding the Changing World of Work*

• *Outsourced: 12 New Rules for Running Your Career in an Interconnected World*

• *The Quantum Leap Strategy*

• *Resistance: Moving Beyond the Barriers to Change*

• *Service Excellence!**

• *Smart Moves: A Crash Course on Merger Integration Management**

• *A Survival Guide to the Stress of Organizational Change**

• *Team ReConstruction: Building a High Performance Work Group During Change**

• *Teamwork: The Team Member Handbook**

• *you^2: A High-Velocity Formula for Multiplying Your Personal Effectiveness in Quantum Leaps*

*Training program also available. Please call 800-992-5922 for more information on our training or international rights and foreign translations.

Survival Training for the Stress of Organizational Change

Change always stresses the organization, and that stress carries a big price tag. You keep paying people full salary, but essentially end up with part-time employees because they're distracted, less productive, and generally weaker performers. Since we can't stop change, it's very important for the workforce to learn how to handle it more effectively.

This inspiring and thought provoking program reveals how people's common reactions to change typically increase their stress level instead of reducing it. Participants learn how to reframe the situation, how to avoid the "15 basic mistakes," plus how to manage their emotions for the good of both themselves and the organization.

Agenda
Module 1: Diagnostic Tool Kit
Module 2: Instant Alignment
Module 3: Plug Into Your Job
Module 4: Survival Plan
Module 5: Survival Guide Prescriptions

Key Objectives
- Improve operating effectiveness
- Harness the energy from pressure in order to drive productivity
- Remain focused on business in stressful situations

Topics Addressed
- "Basic Mistakes" that increase stress levels
- How to align with the organization's business reason for change
- Developing a stress survival plan to reduce the stress you create for yourself

Primary Result
Participants learn how they often cause their own stress unnecessarily, plus receive guidelines on how to reduce stress while increasing their productivity and overall quality of work life.

A SURVIVAL GUIDE TO

THE STRESS OF

ORGANIZATIONAL CHANGE

1-49 copies	_____ copies at $6.95 each
50-99 copies	_____ copies at $6.50 each
100-999 copies	_____ copies at $5.95 each
1,000-4,999 copies	_____ copies at $5.75 each
5,000-9,999 copies	_____ copies at $5.50 each
10,000 or more copies	_____ copies at $5.25 each

Please reference
special customer number 6F6A
when ordering.

Name _____

Job Title _____

Organization _____

Address _____

Country _____ Zip Code _____

Phone _____ Fax _____

Email _____

Purchase order number (if applicable) _____

*Applicable sales tax, shipping and handling charges
will be added. Prices subject to change.
Orders less than $250 require prepayment.
Orders of $250 or more may be invoiced.

☐ Check Enclosed   ☐ Please Invoice*

☐ VISA   ☐ MasterCard   ☐ AMERICAN EXPRESS

Name on Card _____

Card Number _____ Expiration Date _____

Signature _____ Date _____

TO ORDER
By Phone: 800-992-5922
Online: www.pritchettnet.com
Call for our mailing address or fax number.

PRITCHETT
Dallas, Texas